A TRIBUTE TO THE PLYMOUTH LIFEBOATS

Arthur L. Clamp

Prince Consort Lifeboat
This drawing shows crowds welcoming the arrival in Plymouth of the new *Prince Consort* lifeboat in February, 1862, having been carried free of charge on the railway from London. It had ten oars, was provided with a launching carriage and saw service here until 1873. It was launched eleven times and saved sixty people.

This version of the book is virtually as originally published.
There are now additional pages at the back providing information about the author.
On page 2 a promise is made that this booklet will raise money for lifeboats; this will be honoured.

The republishing project is being managed by Arthur's grandson, Steven Gibson. We aim to find all the research that he was involved in publishing, preserving it for the next generation as part of 'The Clamp Collection'.

INTRODUCTION

This illustrated booklet is planned for the general reader and visitor to the city and not to the lifeboat enthusiast who would probably require more details about the lifeboats, their crews and the great many rescues that have taken place since a station was established in Plymouth in 1803.

Plymouth has been a very large port for hundreds of years for naval and merchant shipping and now for increasing leisure craft filling its many marinas. Almost all the lifeboats that have served on this station are shown in this booklet but unfortunately very few records remain from the time when the first two boats were in service from 1803 to about 1820. The station was also closed from 1825 to 1840. From time to time temporary boats have come into service and various small inshore craft have also been used. Some of these are not included in this title. This is not to say that they did not play any part in the rescue services.

The Royal National Lifeboat Institution was established on 4th March, 1824, by Sir William Hillary whose object was to set up a national lifeboat service. A branch was formed in Plymouth in 1825 and a 10 oared rowing lifeboat was recorded being kept at Cawsand but no further information about her has so far been found. Since the arrival of the *Prince Consort* many details of the different lifeboats are available in Plymouth and at the RNLI centre at Poole, Dorset.

This booklet is a tribute to the great many local people who have risked life and limb in responding to hundreds of calls from mariners and others in distress in the waters many miles around Plymouth. There does not seem to be any let up in these calls although the nature of many of them have changed through the steady increase of pleasure sailing and yachting and the unforeseen risks some visitors take when walking along steep cliffs or clambering down to normally inaccessible beaches and sometimes being cut off by the tide.

Although almost all modern vessels are now equipped with a variety of navigational aids human error still plays a part coupled with changing weather conditions when ships get into difficulty and the need for an efficient rapid response time by the lifeboat service is as much required today as ever.

There have been many changes in the lifeboats serving the station from the days when they had sails and were rowed by their crews having on some occasions been towed out into the Sound by one of the Dockyard tugs. The safety of the crew is now more paramount than in the earlier days, their training and equipment is much more thorough and reliable and the response times when calls are made have been considerably reduced with the help of telephones and mobile phones held by some of the crew. The 194 years of lifeboat service at Plymouth less the period when the station was closed is a great tribute to the many volunteers who have manned the lifeboats and to the concerns of local people about the safety of those on the sea.

ACKNOWLEDGEMENTS

I am greatly indebted to many people for assisting me in the preparation of this booklet and for allowing me to consult their records from which many of the facts about the Plymouth lifeboat service originate. Among these are the retired and present members of the crew who allowed me to see the station's records and photographic albums, their own photographs, certificates and medals and to suggest other sources of information.

John Dare and Cyril Alcock, now retired, must be mentioned together with Dereck Studden and Tony Owens of the present crew with others who made various suggestions about where information made be found. Some of this came from the Plymouth city library, Jeff Morris of the Lifeboat Enthusiasts Society and Mrs. Kathy Hole. It was the staff of the new lifeboat shop in the Barbican who suggested that a record of Plymouth's station should be made from which an income for the R.N.L.I. will accrue.

Arthur L. Clamp,
203 Elburton Road,
Plymouth, Devon, PL9 8HX

Prince Consort Lifeboat

Seen here on the beach with its horse drawn carriage, it was built by Forrestt of Limehouse, London, at a cost of £80. It was the gift of Miss Burdett Coutts, of London, and was a typically built lifeboat of that period when stations around the country were starting to provide a rescue service for mariners under the Royal National Lifeboat Institution.

CLEMENCY LIFEBOAT 1873-1886

This ten oared boat came on station on 30th May, 1873, and undertook eleven launches saving thirty-eight lives during its service.

It was later kept in the new lifeboat house at the Camber and was launched down rails into the water and sometimes towed by one of the new steam tugs in the Dockyard close to the scene of a boat in distress.

It was the gift of Mr. and Mrs. J. G. Hubbard and was presented to Captain Ward, R.N., on behalf of the RNLI. The crew were treated to a tea the previous evening in the harbour master's watch house.

Like other lifeboats it was built in Limehouse, London, and cost £294 and the cost of getting it to Plymouth by rail was defrayed by the G.W.R.

Its first call out was to the *John Barbour* in late February, 1874, when she broke away from her anchor and drifted into an Italian brig. The lifeboat crew managed to get a tow aboard to a waiting tug which separated the two vessels so averting them going aground.

There were other minor rescues from time to time and then in October, 1881, a Dutch vessel carrying teak was driven ashore in Mount Batten Bay the *Clemency* stood by until a steam tug came which was to have pulled the vessel away. However, this was not possible so the crew of eleven were saved by being taken by the lifeboat to the tug.

A strong gale in January, 1885, caused the vessel *Wellington* of Nova Scotia to send up distress signals off Plymouth and under coxswain Lucock the *Clemency* was launched to the vessel anchored between the Mewstone and the coast. With help from the Yealm lifeboat the *Wellington* was towed into the Yealm estuary where the lifeboat had to remain for twelve hours before being towed back to Plymouth by a steam tug. She later towed the *Wellington* again which had got into difficulty this time at Millbay.

Three Pictures

The upper one is an artist's drawing of a lifeboat of this period showing its crew struggling against the power of the waves and the middle one is a line drawing of 1873 when Plymouth's waterfront was awash with waves and debris from ships caught under the lee of the Hoe.

Coxswain William Teel's gravestone in a Plymouth cemetery recording his links with the lifeboat service is the lower picture. When he retired in 1884 he was awarded the RNLI silver medal for his long service at Plymouth. He was succeeded by coxswain John Lucock.

Escape Lifeboat in service 1886 to 1898

The boat was built by Forrestt of London at a cost of £327; it had ten oars and it was the gift of Miss Lucy Harris of London. It was launched fifteen times and rescued seven people from the barquetine *Kate* of Greenwich which was loaded with logwood going ashore at Mount Batten bay. In December, 1890, it went to the assistance of ss *Nepaul* which ran aground on rocks near the Shagstone. The crew are pictured here in April, 1887, wearing the standard cork lifejacket. The lifeboat is on the launching rails of the slipway at the Camber, Millbay Docks.

ELIZA AVINS LIFEBOAT

This was in service at Plymouth from 1898 to 1922 and was the legacy of Mr. John Avins of Birmingham. It was 37 feet in length, had ten oars, and was built in the yard of Thames Ironworks for £699. A new boat house and launching slipway was built at the Camber for her for £427 10s. which can still be seen today.

Having no engine and dependent upon wind and oar the boat was sometimes towed out into the Sound by one of the dockyard tugs. She was launched 27 times and 27 lives were saved through her efforts. It is recorded that David Mumford took over as coxswain in 1901.

In November, 1902, she was called to the vessel *Snowdrop* a brigantine anchored in the Sound with a crew of two. The coxswain and some of the lifeboat crew managed to get on board and get a line to a tug which took her into harbour.

Another year of her active service was in 1920 when a French vessel carrying logwood lost her sails in hurricane winds and hit the Breakwater. Flares were sent up and the lifeboat stood by taking on the French crew although one was swept away.

1912 Boxing Day Storm

The left picture shows the *Eliza Alvins* stuck on rocks when attempting to go to the aid of the schooner *Ottawa* in Jennycliff Bay. She was one of many vessels caught in the great storm on Boxing Day in 1912. Five crew were rescued and the lifeboat refloated on the next high tide.

Three Sails and Crew

The location of the lower picture has not been identified but the *Eliza Alvins* is under sail with her crew probably on a training exercise.

BROTHERS FREEMAN LIFEBOAT 1922-1926

This was the last of the ten oared lifeboats that served at Plymouth crewed by very courageous men exposed to the elements and rowing the boat in often very stormy waters. The steam tugs working in the Dockyard would sometimes help by towing the lifeboat close to a vessel in distress and then slipping the tow line to allow the boat to get in closer. The *Brothers Freeman* served here for only four years being launched two times and rescuing two people. It was replaced by a new generation of motor driven boats.

The old lifeboats were housed in the small lifeboat station at the Camber, Millbay Docks, and were launched manually down rails on a ramp with the crew in position, oars raised and themselves wearing the old style cork life jackets. The coxswain took up his position at the rudder and all strained at the oars to get the heavy boat seawards.

This lifeboat had seen service at Littlehampton; it was built in 1904, was 35 feet in length, and came on station on 6th September, 1922. The illustration below is thought to be *Brothers Freeman* as it dates from the early 1920s and like almost all other lifeboats was from time to time involved in fund raising activities.

In April, 1923, she was called out to assist the Milford Haven based s.s. *Unicorn* which was carrying a cargo of bricks to Jersey from Bridgwater. The vessel encountered heavy storms and seas 3 miles south west of Ramehead and it was thought that she had gone down. The *Brothers Freeman* was towed out of the Sound by one of the Dockyard steam tugs and rescued two of her five crew from a small boat launched just before the vessel went down.

The departure of this lifeboat from the Plymouth station brought to an end the era of rowed lifeboats and the extremely hard and courageous work that the crews had to do to get to scenes of distress. There were many awards for gallantry during the early years because of crews having to face very hazardous sea conditions in an open boat.

On Sea and Land

A typical scene when Plymouth was served by lifeboats equipped with ten oars and sails. There was no cover for the crew who were exposed to the full force of any storms. On land the lifeboat is being hauled towards Stonehouse bridge as part of a fund raising event with a long handled net held out for money. Note the massive wheels and carriage for carrying the lifeboat.

Robert and Marcella Beck Lifeboat in service from 1926 to 1943 and 1947 to 1952

This boat was requisitioned for war service so making a break in its presence at Plymouth. It was launched thirty-six times and rescued seventy lives and was the legacy of Mr. R. A. Beck of Worthing. A Barnett class vessel, sixty feet in length, non-self righter, it was powered by two 80 hp petrol engines giving a top speed of 9.5 knots. It came on station on 1st July, 1926, costing £14,536 to build. The crew of Bert Sleeman, Walter Crowther, coxswain, Arthur Banham, mechanic, Arthur Foot, Fred Fowler, Walter Lillicrap, Len Holmes, George Stanbury, John Hignett and Ernie Curtis are seen here in its last period of service. Coxswains Eagles and Jim Roach also served on this lifeboat.

MINISTRE ANSEELE 1943-1946

The war years brought particular problems to the lifeboat service often interrupting the crewing of boats, restricting the coastal areas in which they would normally enter and, in the case of Plymouth, the requisitioning of its lifeboat the *Robert and Marcella Beck* for war service around Iceland. Fortunately the Belgian boat *Ministre Anseele* was found drifting in the English Channel and she was brought to Plymouth and placed on station on 21st March, 1943, serving here until April, 1946, when she was returned to Belgium.

She was launched six times and saved five lives in addition to giving some assistance to allied ships uncertain of local waters. To date no photograph of her has been found of her possibly because of the restrictive use of cameras around the sensitive naval port of Plymouth. Unlike the peacetime lifeboat crews there were more changes during this period than normal due to call up.

She was first called out in August, 1943, to the Renny Rocks where three men were rescued having become stranded after trying to get their boat off the rocks. In 1945 she gave assistance to the liberty ship *James E. Layne* which was being towed towards the shore sinking in Whitesands Bay. Further details are alongside the picture below of this call out. Although only two rescues are recorded for the war years, there were many more incidents involving military planes and ships which were not reported in the local press or made public in any way.

Peace came in 1945 and the lifeboat is recorded saving a motor boat *Three Brothers* with her crew of three in February, 1946. The *Ministre Anseele* was then returned to Belgian and her place was taken by another temporary boat *The Brothers* which stood in while a major overhaul took place on the *Robert and Marcella Beck* before she returned to serve Plymouth for a few more years.

James E. Layne
This U.S. liberty ship of 10,000 tons carrying a general cargo was hit by a German submarine near the Eddystone on 21st March, 1945. The *Ministre Anseele* was called out and found that she was already in tow towards Whitesands Bay where she later sank. The lifeboat retrieved two life rafts and took them into Plymouth.

Allied Forces
In the war years many vessels of allied forces used Plymouth as a port. They were unfamiliar with its waters and often called for assistance from the lifeboat. A United States Landing Ship Tank has hit the Breakwater seen here in December, 1945, a casualty of such a situation.

Thomas Forehead and Mary Rowse Lifeboat, 1952-1974

The upper view shows the naming ceremony in Millbay Docks in March, 1952, crewed by Albert Holmes, Walter Crowther, Tom Keane, Nic Carter, Sid Harris, Arthur Banham, Fred Fowler, Bert Sleeman and Len Holmes. An inspector from Poole is also aboard. The boat was built at Cowes by J. Samuel White, a 52 ft. Barnet class, self righter. It cost £30,857 and had two 60 hp diesel engines.

The lower view shows her on the way across the Sound to Mashford's boat yard, her last journey in these waters before she was passed on to another station. Cyril Alcock and John Dare crewed her for this short journey.

Crew of the Thomas Forehead and Mary Rowse II
This was the crew for the years 1967-68 seen here at Millbay Docks. They are from left to right John Sheldon, Danny Biscombe, Albert Holmes, bowman, Fred Fowler, Bill Rogers, Peter White, coxswain, John Dare, second coxswain, and John Keane.

THOMAS FOREHEAD AND MARY ROWSE II LIFEBOAT

This was the first of a new and modern class of lifeboat which was on station from 1947 to 1987. It was built in the Cowes yard of Messrs. Groves and Guttridge; steel hulled, a Waveney class vessel, self righter and 44 feet in length. The vessel was powered by two 260 hp diesel engines which gave her a top speed of 16 knots and cost £100,000 to build.

She arrived in Plymouth in May, 1974, and was christened by the Duchess of Kent on 17th June, 1974. There were 181 launches and 91 lives were saved through her crew's efforts and the increased efficiency and response time of this new class of lifeboat. Her last journey was a short one to Mashford's boatyard for a survey but she did not return on station.

Throughout her service she was engaged in all kinds of sea and coastal responses undertaking some spectacular rescues under the most difficult of sea conditions. Members of her crew were awarded medals and certificates examples of which are shown on the rescue pages of this booklet.

In February, 1978, she was called out to the fishing vessel *Elly Gerda* which was taken into Looe harbour. Acting coxswain Pat Marshall and Cyril Alcock were awarded bronze medals for their gallantry in this service. A French fishing vessel *Saint Simeon* was reported sinking nineteen miles off the Lizard in February, 1985. Details of this dramatic rescue are on page 21. Numerous other less dramatic rescues are listed in the station's record book all pointing to the determination of the crew to render help whatever the circumstances of those in distress.

Plymouth's new lifeboat due on Friday

PLYMOUTH'S new self-righting lifeboat, costing more than £80,000, is due in the port on Friday. The District Inspector of Lifeboats, Lieut-Com Roy Portchmouth, and coxswain John Dare, together with a crew from Plymouth, will be collecting the boat from Cowes, Isle of Wight.

They will be making an extended passage to Plymouth via St Peter Port in the Channel Islands.

The new boat, to be named the Thomas Forehead and Mary Rowse II, has a 44ft steel hull and belongs to the Waveney class, based on an American design modified for the Royal National Lifeboat Institution.

The new vessel has been undergoing extensive trials off the Isle of Wight, where she was built.

Lifeboat tows in ketch

Plymouth lifeboat, the Thomas Forehead and Mary Rowse the Second, put to sea yesterday to tow in a 50ft ketch that had broken down eight miles from Looe.

The Amy M, with four people aboard, was at first taken in tow by a fishing boat after her engines failed. The Plymouth lifeboat completed the tow, taking the launch into Looe. Nobody was hurt.

Thomas Forehead and Mary Rowse II Lifeboat

Both photographs were taken in Millbay Docks the upper in November, 1980, with Mike Foster and Cyril Alcock aboard and below can be seen the Admiral, Flag Officer and their wives being taken on a short trip around the Sound in June, 1984, accompanied by Tiny Parker, Cyril Alcock, and Phil Reed. John Dare is at the wheel.

On the Thomas Forehead and Mary Rowse II Lifeboat
The crew are assembled here in 1988 on an appeal run for funds for the present lifeboat. They are Frank Parker, Dereck Studden, Steve Ray, Mike Smalldon, Archie Roberts, Cyril Alcock, John Dare, coxswain, Pat Marshall, Ray Jago, Keith Rimmer and Fred Jackson all suitably dressed for the occasion.

CITY OF PLYMOUTH LIFEBOAT

This is the present lifeboat which came on station on 26th January, 1988, equipped with the latest navigational aids including radar, Decca navigator, VHF and MF, auto direction finder and echo sounder, carrying a seating crew of seven and reaching 18 knots with her two 485 hp diesel engines the fastest speed yet for any Plymouth lifeboat. She is GRP hulled, 52 feet in length, an Arun class vessel, self righter and fitted out by Souters of Cowes bringing the total cost of construction to £592,478. So far she has been launched 194 times and rescued 71 lives from all kinds of large and small vessels some well out to sea, others close inshore and people stranded on cliffs.

The increase in leisure craft over the past two decades has changed to some extent the nature of many of her rescues. More people are venturing onto the sea often with little knowledge or experience and in some cases ill equipped to face changing weather conditions even with detailed weather forecasts being made.

The first rescue for this lifeboat came on the same day she came on station when she went to the aid of a fishing vessel about 6 miles off Rame Head. It had a crew of two and the vessel was towed into Plymouth. A wind surfer was in difficulties off Stoke beach in July, 1989. The man was exhausted and the inflatable boat was launched which took him to the beach at Stoke. Later that year a young person on board a training vessel had appendicitis and was taken by the lifeboat to a waiting ambulance in Plymouth. In January, 1990, the lifeboat took in tow a yacht which had lost its steering controls in the marina at Clovelly Bay and a man was rescued from his houseboat on the same call out. Some typical entries in the station's log book are: January, 1993: Gave help to the fishing vessel *Calypso*. April 1993: Gave help to two girls and a dog cut off by the tide. August, 1996: Launched on service to the fishing vessel *William* broken down south of Looe Island. September 1996: Launched on service for persons cut off by tide at Sharrow Point, Whitesand Bay. November, 1996: Launched on service to red flares reported 5 miles south east of east end of the Breakwater. November 1996: Launched on service to sick man on fishing vessel *Grietje*. May 1997: Launched on service for two persons cut off by tide at Stoke Beach.

The lifeboat is maintained in a state of readiness by Dereck Studden, full time mechanic, and throughout the year various exercises and public relation trips are undertaken to ensure that when a call is made for assistance the crew and boat are in maximum readiness and are able to respond as quickly as possible.

Brass Plaque on Lifeboat
RNLB *City of Plymouth*
named in Sutton Harbour
on 15th April, 1988,
by
Mrs. Jeanne Parish,
Lady Mayoress of Plymouth.

Brass Plaque on Lifeboat
The cost of this lifeboat
was provided by the citizens of
Plymouth together with the
bequests of George Wilfred Glass,
Phyllis Maud Lyneham,
Margaret Scott,
Dorothy Janet Gertrude Singleton
and other gifts and legacies.

Brass Plaque on Lifeboat
The cost of the portable VHF
radio aboard RNLB *City of
Plymouth* was met by
donations from the family
and friends in memory of
John Stallard.

City of Plymouth lifeboat at her mooring in Millbay Marina in May, 1997.

Crew of the City of Plymouth Lifeboat

They are assembled in front of the lifeboat house at Millbay Docks in May, 1997, ready for an exercise run. They are Paul Millet, Tony Owen, Mike West, Dereck Studden, mechanic, Keith Rimmer, Dave Milford, John West, Rob Anderson, Dave Ellis and Pat Marshall, coxswain. Below is seen the lifeboat having just left its Millbay mooring on the same day speeding out across the inshore waters of the Sound. Note the former lifeboat house in the background.

GRP hulled McLachlan A-509 Inshore Rescue Boat

This was on station from July, 1972, to August, 1980, and was kept at Millbay. It is seen here with John Dare, Clifton Andrews and Keith Rimmer and it was involved in one rescue of a boy at Bovisand who had fallen down the cliffs and cut off by the rising tide.

Relief Lifeboat Lloyds

Relief boats are called on station from time to time when the main lifeboat is away for repairs or undergoing modifications. This one was at Plymouth for about eight weeks in 1968 and is seen here at the Barbican regatta crewed by Danny Biscombe, Bill Rogers, Tom Keane, John Dare, Peter White, coxswain, and Fred Fowler.

RNLI Bronze Medal
Awarded to Cyril Alcock in 1978 for his part in the rescue of crew from the trawler *Elly Gerda*.

1942
An outstanding service was carried out on the 19th January when in a very rough sea a Sunderland Flying Boat of the Australian Royal Air Force was carried on to the rocks under the cliffs in Jennycliffe Bay. The two men on board the flying boat were rescued. For this service Coxswain Walter Crowther received the Institution's bronze medal for gallantry, and each of the eight members of his crew the Institution's thanks inscribed on vellum.

The medals were presented by H.R.H. the Duke of Kent President of the Institution. This was the Duke of Kent's last service to the Institution, as on the 25th August he was killed in an air accident on active service.

Extract from the station's records book.

British Empire Medal
This was awarded to Cyril Alcock for his many years of service with the Plymouth lifeboats.

Rescue off Black Rock
This painting was presented to John Dare, coxswain, on 10th November, 1990, when he retired from the lifeboat crew. An air sea rescue helicopter is undertaking a high line rescue from the grounded yacht. Pat Marshall and Mike Kitts went on board from the *City of Plymouth* lifeboat to assist in this operation.

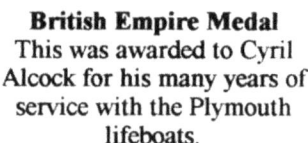

From: CAPTAIN P. KEITH-WELSH, ROYAL NAVY

CAPTAIN OF DOCKYARD
& QUEEN'S HARBOUR MASTER
H.M. Dockyard, DEVONPORT
Telephone: Plymouth 53740, ext. C.B.5 3062/994

15th July, 1968.

Trawler PATRICK

Dear Sir

The Master of the tug ALSATIAN tells me that members of your lifeboat's crew gave valuable assistance onboard his vessel in fighting the fire in the Trawler PATRICK on the night of Saturday 13th July.

2. I would like to express my warm thanks to all who took part in this 'combined operation' which was a fine example of the Comradeship of the sea that Lifeboat Crews do so much to foster.

Yours sincerely,

Capt. R.N.

The Secretary,
Plymouth Lifeboat,
131 Underwood Road,
Plympton,
PLYMOUTH.

Copies to: Commander-in-Chief, Plymouth.
Mr. Penberthy, Master of Tug ALSATIAN.

City of Plymouth Lifeboat
Fred Jackson and Mike Kitts are suitably kitted out for this fund raising launch in the early 1990s.

Lifeboat Crews
The opening of the Plymouth boat show on the Hoe in 1978 was supported by crew members Mike Bluett, Gerald MacManus, Mike Foster, *Miss Plymouth Lifeboat*, Ivor Lovering, John Dare and Cyril Allcock all smiling for the occasion.

Visiting Dignitary
Vice-Admiral Sir Robert Gerken is welcomed aboard the lifeboat by John Dare and Pat Marshall in June, 1984, at the landing stage at Admiralty House.

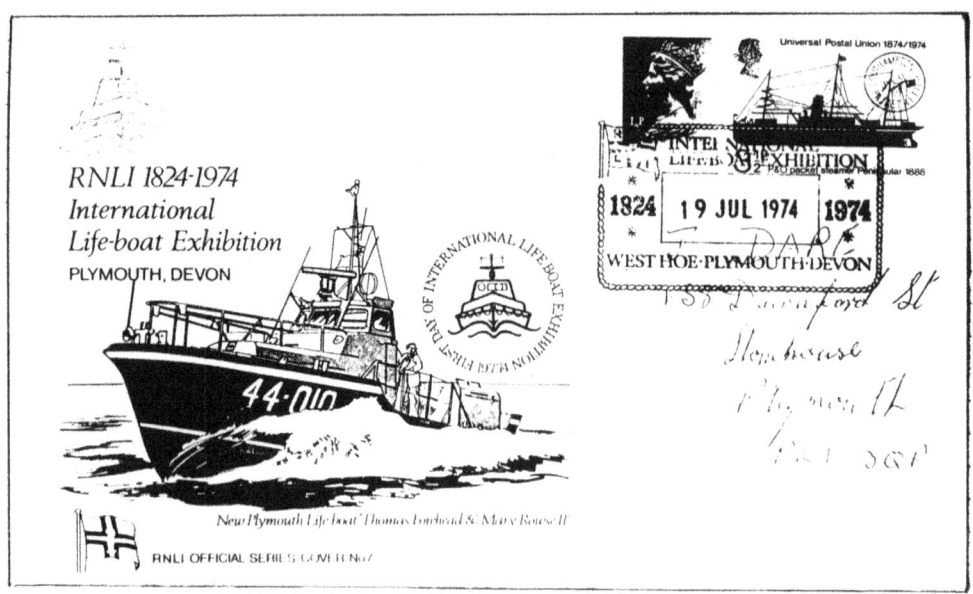

First Day Cover
This was issued to commemorate the first International Lifeboat Exhibition staged in Plymouth from the 19th July to the 17th August, 1974. It was opened by the Duke of Kent, President of the R.N.L.I.

Duke of Edinburgh
H.R.H. Prince Phillip visited the lifeboat station then at Princess Pier, Millbay. In view are Mr. Hicks, honorary secretary, P. White, F. Amos, W. Rogers, T. Keane, D. Biscombe, F. Fowler and J. Dare.

Inshore Lifeboat
This 18 ft. Hatch boat saw service here from September, 1968, to November, 1971. D. Fowler, D. Biscombe and C. Alcock are crewing her in this view taken in Plymouth Sound.

Patrons: Her Majesty The Queen
Her Majesty Queen Elizabeth, The Queen Mother
President: H.R.H. Princess Marina, Duchess of Kent

ROYAL NATIONAL LIFE-BOAT INSTITUTION
Founded 1824. Supported entirely by Voluntary Contributions

TREASURER: THE DUKE OF NORTHUMBERLAND, K.G., D.C.L.

PORT OF PLYMOUTH BRANCH
President: The Earl of Mount Edgcumbe.
Chairman: Mr. Crispin Gill.
Honorary Treasurer: Mr. W. A. K. Frost,
Barclays Bank Limited, Princess Square, Armada Way, Plymouth.
Honorary Secretary: Mr. R. H. E. Sainsbury,
131 Underwood Road, Plympton. Tel: Home 37506. Office 60151.

Plymouth Life-Boat Crew at 1st January

```
Coxswain      -  P.L. White
2nd Coxswain  -  J. Dare
Mechanic      -  C. Alcock
Asst. Mech.   -  T. Keane
Crew             F. Amos
                 D. Biscombe
                 M. Keane
                 J. Sheldon

Reserves      -  R. Jago
                 R. Cotterell
                 D. Dinham
                 P. Marshall
```

Honorary Secretary

Plymouth Lifeboat Crew List in 1997

P. Marshall, coxswain
K. Rimmer, second coxswain
D. Studden, mechanic
A. Owen, assistant mechanic
P. Millett
D. Milford, deputy second coxswain and EM
M. Kitt
J. West
S. Marshall
W. Stephens
C. Marshall
M. West
R. Anderson
C. Baccus
D. Ellis

Officials
P. Willerton, station honorary secretary
M. West, deputy launching authority
M. East, deputy launching authority
A. Melhuish, deputy launching authority
V. Stimson, deputy launching authority

Brixham coastguards coordinate all the rescues in this area.

Two Crew Lists
The first list names the lifeboat crew in the late 1970s with officials of the station. The second list dates from 1997 with a much larger number of local volunteers together with their phone numbers and, in many cases, mobile phone numbers, a sign of the age and the way communications have developed. A rapid response can now be made for call outs.

Rescue of a Flying Boat
This occurred on Saturday, 31st May, 1986, when one of two wartime Catalina flying boats hit a marker buoy upon coming to land in Plymouth Sound. The photograph captures the rescue work on the damaged plane having just flown across the Atlantic for the commemoration of the sixty-seventh anniversary of the first crossing by a flying boat. The *City of Plymouth* lifeboat commenced pumping water from the partially sinking flying boat then towed it slowly to the safety of a boat ramp at Mount Batten.

Man swept overboard is rescued by lifeboat

A MAN who was swept overboard from a cruiser when it was being towed into Plymouth last night by the Plymouth lifeboat was rescued in rough weather by the lifeboat crew.

The man, Mr. Howard Ellis, aged 56, chief surveyor of the Blue Circle Cement Group, of Mark Beech, Kent, was on passage from Fowey to Plymouth on the last day of a charter cruise in a Plymouth boat.

He was travelling with Mr. Geoffrey Matthews, aged 40, of Dowing-road, Haselldon, Norwich. The two men, both married, were on a week's holiday. They are both experienced sailors.

In the Duke of Cornwall Hotel, Plymouth, last night, after changing from wet clothing, Mr. Ellis told his story.

He said they had chartered a cabin cruiser which had been built in Plymouth and was owned by Plymouth Sound Yacht Services, Turnchapel. He praised the boat for standing up to the rough weather, and said he had never been caught out before by such a quick change in weather conditions.

February 1978

PLYMOUTH lifeboatmen talked last night of the "miracle" trawler rescue off the South Cornish coast 24 hours earlier which had kept them at sea for 14 hours in a blizzard.

The lifeboat shadowed the Teignmouth - registered trawler Elly Gerda, listing with a 40-ton load of mackerel, until she reached the safety of Looe Harbour late on Wednesday night.

It was the second time that 31-year-old Patrick Marshall, the second coxswain and a Ministry of Defence worker, had taken the lifeboat out since his promotion from assistant mechanic last month.

"It was one of the longest services we have been called to give for some time," he said. "Eighteen hours was the longest."

Mr. Marshall praised the "first-class seamanship" of trawler skipper Peter Vickerstaff in slipping his vessel into Looe with only six or seven inches clearance.

Rescue off Looe
This 1947-48 photograph records this pleasure boat rescue undertaken by Tom Keane, Fred Fowler, Arthur Banham, Walter Crowther, coxswain, Nic Carter and Albert Holmes.

Rescueing Canoeists
Assistance at nightime is being given here by the crew of the lifeboat *Thomas Forehead and Mary Rowse II* in Plymouth Sound.

Nightmare of crew's fight for survival

THE SKIPPER of the French trawler abandoned during fierce storms told today of their nightmare hours as they battled to get to the safety of the Plymouth lifeboat.

Jean-Claude Cardron, 40, said over breakfast with his crew at the Royal Fleet Club, Devonport : " We got into our own little lifeboat. Then we left the St Simeon by holding on to a rope which we let out bit by bit as we approached the Plymouth lifeboat. Then we cut the line. It was about midnight. The lifeboat men were superb.

" They reached out and brought us on board. We talked a little with the captain who asked us if we were OK. We were very relieved to be saved. The conditions were very dangerous."

Crew member Herve Levourch, 37, said : " We were all very shaken by the experience."

February 1985

Landing survivors from the *Saint Simeon* at night.

Weather Beaten Captain
The French skipper of the Saint Simeon, Claude Cardron, reaches the safety of the lifeboat station on 15th February, 1985, seen here with Ian Baker, coastguard and others.

Award of Certificates
Vellum certificates were presented to Raymond Jago, John Dare, Cyril Alcock and Keith Rimmer in October, 1985, for their part in the rescue of the crew from the French trawler.

Return from a Successful Rescue

Raymond Jago, John Dare, 1st coxswain, Pat Marshall, 2nd coxswain, Fred Jackson and Dereck Studden, are seen here on their return from the successful rescue and assistance given to the M.V. *Kaprifol* further details of which are in the newspaper article below.

A MAN was washed into the sea off Plymouth today in a rescue drama involving a freighter ferry stricken by an engine-room fire.

The lorry driver was pulled from the water by lifeboatmen and taken ashore with another passenger from the 9,000-ton roll-on, roll-off ferry MV Kaprifol, which has been at the centre of a seamen's dispute.

The Spanish bound vessel was off Rame Head on its way out of Millbay Docks battling through heavy seas in a Force 9 gale when the fire broke out.

The lorry driver was trying to climb down a ladder into the lifeboat when he was dragged into the swirling waters. Later a full evacuation of the ship was halted when the blaze was put out.

Today the two men brought ashore were resting and recovering from their ordeal at the Royal Fleet Club, Devonport.

The ferry later restarted its engines and headed back into Millbay.

Plymouth lifeboat coxswain John Dare said they had got one man off safely when a second lorry driver started climbing down the side of the ship.

15th December 1986

THEIR SKILL and courage in the face of hurricane force winds and mountainous seas in an attempt to help the stricken Danish coaster, Merc Enterprise, 20 miles off Bolt Head in January, has won bravery awards for Coxswain John Dare and crew of the Plymouth lifeboat.

The bronze medal of the Royal National Lifeboat Institution goes to Mr Dare and medal service certificates to the other six members of the crew.

The citation goes on: "For an admirable execution of duty in the face of frightening conditions, the bronze medal of the RNLI has been awarded to Coxswain John Dare."

On January 16, Plymouth lifeboat went out to assist the coaster, which was in serious difficulties in hurricane-force winds, and, says the citation: "Very rough seas were accompanied by driving rain, and the coxswain and crew found themselves up to their waists in water in the wheelhouse.

16th January 1974

Bronze Medal Award

This certificate awarded by the R.N.L.I. in June, 1974, to John Dare, coxswain, provides a glowing testimony to the courage of the lifeboat crews who, over the years, have undertaken many similar courageous rescues as this one.

Fund Raising
Senior girls of Courtlands School, Widey, raised £55 during their Christmas term in 1984 for R.N.L.I. funds seen here being acknowledged by Cyril Alcock, John Dare and Frank Jago aboard the *Thomas Forehead and Mary Rowse II* lifeboat.

Barometer Presentation
Cyril Alcock is receiving this gift given by Jim Bryant owner of the Plymouth Sea Angling Centre where the presentation took place. It went on display in the Princess Pier, Millbay, lifeboat station and will be placed on display in the present one.

Long Service Award
The late Frank Parker is seen here receiving his long service award in 1995 from Brian Miles, National Director of the R.N.L.I., watched by ex-crew member Brian Bellamy.

Former Lifeboat House
The small limestone lifeboat house and slipway still stand at the Camber, Millbay Docks, from where the earlier lifeboats were housed and launched. It is now surrounded by much larger and later buildings and is part of the Royal Marines complex at the Long Room.

Princess Pier
This was the lifeboat house for a few years built on the Princess Pier, Millbay Docks, in 1976 from monies collected locally. The developments here necessitated a move for the station until the present one was opened.

Lifeboat House
This is Plymouth's present lifeboat house at Millbay Docks which was opened in 1993. A former customs house, it has three storeys, is octagonal in shape and was converted partly through a bequest of Mrs. Eugenie Boucher. It stands close to where the lifeboat is moored and has good facilities for the crew when dressing to get ready to go to a rescue.

Arthur L. Clamp – the man behind the books

Arthur Leslie Clamp was a man of boundless energy with a passion for helping others, particularly through his love of history. A printer by trade, he started his career in a printing company before moving his family from Exeter to Plymouth to teach at the Plymouth College of Art and Design, where he eventually became the Head of the Printing Department.

Arthur with his five children.

A Devoted Family Man

Despite his love of teaching, Arthur prioritised his family, always making it home by 5:30pm for tea. He and his wife, Rosemary, raised five children: Susan, Angela, Elizabeth, David, and Steven. Arthur would often combine his love of family and history by taking his children on Sunday walks, encouraging them to appreciate historical monuments by taking photos or making crayon rubbings of gravestones for his books. The family home at 203 Elburton Road was a hub of activity, with a large garden, featuring a two-storey fort and a makeshift swimming pool.

A Lifelong Learner and Adventurer

Arthur's thirst for knowledge extended beyond history to a deep curiosity about the world. He was passionate about exploring different cultures, traditions, and cuisines, often taking advantage of his long summer holidays as a teacher to travel to places like India, Russia, South America, the middle east and the USA, sometimes bringing one of his children along. This adventurous spirit even influenced his home life, as seen by the short-lived family tradition of steam-cooking vegetables after a trip to Iceland.

History is a prominent feature of family days out

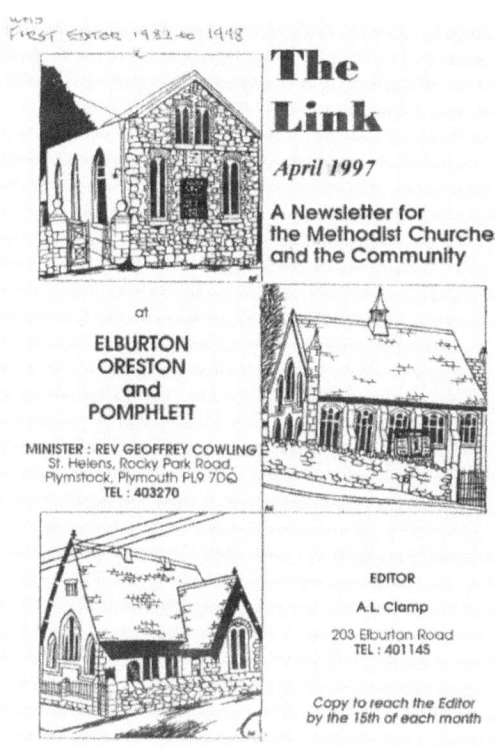

Community and Philanthropic Spirit

His commitment to serving others was evident in his long-standing involvement with the Elburton Methodist Church. He was the Sunday School Superintendent for over 15 years and served as the editor of the wider church's monthly newsletter, "The Link," for a similar duration. After Rosemary's very sad passing, Arthur later remarried and, following a chance encounter with a professor from India, established a connection with a missionary school in Chennai. Together with his new wife, Christine, he co-founded a "Sponsor a Child's Education" program that continues to this day.

*Pictured left – The cover of 'The Link' complete with hand drawn sketches of each church by Angela
Below right – Arthur Clamp promoting his latest book
Below left – Arthur at home with his first wife, Rosemary
Below centre – Arthur on holiday with his second wife, Christine*

A Legacy of Learning and Positivity

Arthur's greatest passion was history, which he brought to life through tireless research, documentation, and the many books he authored. He was driven by a need to "never be stuck in a rut," constantly seeking new experiences, meeting new people, and expanding his knowledge. With a positive attitude and a great sense of humour, he was always ready to help others, leaving a lasting impact on his family and community. His children, Susan, Angela, Elizabeth, David, and Steven, remember him with love and gratitude.

David Clamp, 2025

A Legacy of Local History

Below is the story of how Arthur L Clamp began writing books, in his own words, drafted shortly before he passed away in 2001. I have only made minor alterations to this text, correcting grammatical errors that he did not survive to correct himself. When I first discovered this text, I was shocked to see my name mentioned. It seems that, unbeknownst to me, I shared my first PC with him. I suspect he used it during the day when I was at school, although I do have one memory of sitting with him and showing him how it worked. It has been a pleasure to pick up where he left off and see his books republished and redistributed, and to know that I was part of the story, even back then. It was also fascinating to discover that his pricing structure matches the way I have tried to price the books, with a third going to local sellers and the rest covering printing costs with a little left over for my expenses.

I am his eldest grandson, and it is a privilege to curate his legacy, which we are calling 'The Clamp Collection'. The very last line of the text originally reads "The following pages list all the titles." Sadly, that page is missing and we have no record of all the books he published and knowing that some of those were researched by other authors makes the process of finding them even harder. I look forward to one day completing the collection and seeing them all available again. And maybe, one day, I'll even start writing my own to add to the series. For now, here is his story in his own words.

Steven Gibson, 2025

Writing and Publishing Booklets on Local Topics and Areas

I started this interest in either 1968 or 1969 when living in Woodford. I had by these dates established the Department of Printing and I think I must have been looking for something different to do. The first titles were of A5 size proofed from type set at Clarke, Doble and Brendon, Ltd., Plymouth printers, and then made up into pages and printed at Sawtell and Neilson, Ltd., Totnes.

Then began a slow process of getting them out to shops, etc. which proved to be more time consuming and difficult than actually researching, writing and getting the books into print. However, I persisted and opened a business account with Barclays Bank on the Broadway. I was advised to give it a title so I called it "Westway Publications". There came along another problem, one of storage of paper and finished books which was solved when the family moved to Elburton in 1970.

I changed the printer to Penwell, Ltd., Callington, Cornwall, as he was then just setting up himself and his prices seemed very reasonable. I did not get any of the printers to make up the complete books. I hand folded the flat printed sheets, stitched the books on a small manual table stitcher and trimmed them in a small hand turned guillotine which I bought from someone in Penzance for £40. It was brought up in a van.

The trouble and time going to and fro to Callington was too much so I transferred the printing to PDS Printers, Prince Rock, Plymouth, and I have been with them ever since. Now they are at Plympton which is easy to reach and they fold the flat sheets which was turning out to be a long chore which only saved a small part of the printing costs.

All my first titles were written by myself. I took the photographs and developed them in the loft of the house, the type was set by now on a computer situated in the house at Elburton from which I had collected photographic lengths of text to cut up and law down as pages.

At some point I decided that I would do my own film processing of lith film so I bought a large second hand process camera from Kingsbridge and learnt through trial and error to make line negatives of the text and halftone negatives of the illustrations which proved more difficult than I anticipated. The main problem was trying to keep the developer in the large dish at the correct temperature as any change would affect the developing time. I replaced this old camera with a brand new one bought from Croydon, Surrey, costing £900. This has turned out to be a great asset cutting out an expensive part of the printer's costs and one crucial aspect of the work which I could control.

By the middle 1970s there were many outlets I had contacted in Plymouth, up to Dartmoor, Exeter, around to Torbay, Totnes, Dartmouth and the South Hams. The market for local books was much greater than I had first thought and through getting to know many local people undertaking research themselves had the chance to help and make up books for other people who had in most instances, got together a collection of photographs with some text in a rather muddled way. Through my experience in print I was able to shape up their work and get it into print and in every case I had to pay the printer and let the person have the royalties. In the majority of titles produced in this manner this was another way of producing titles and it did give some profit to my work. However, I must say that in a few cases I lost out by either the other person getting the numbers wrong, not returning any monies from stock I delivered or they thought that more of their books should have been sold.

The print run was usually 1,000 copies and from time to time I have had reprints of 250 copies. It took about ten years to clear the first print run so I always had large stocks in the garage, workshop, etc. The numbers sold during the early years was about 7,000 copies a year increasing to around 9,000 copies and for the whole of the enterprise about 500,000 have been sold. The booklets have become part of the local scene and many people collect them, shops regularly order copies and I go around certain areas month by month restocking or replacing titles as necessary.

During the past year or so I have started setting the text on a Packard Bell PC, something which I should have done some years back. I share it with Steven Gibson, my grandson. There appears to be no end to the market for local books, but I could not earn a regular income because of the long time it takes to sell stock.

However, now exceeding 100 titles made up mainly of A4 twenty-four page booklets, some folded guides, with selling prices set with a third going to the shop which is the trade custom, the original idea has been quite successful and could go on for ever.

Apart from monetary benefits, however spasmodically these might be, I have learnt a lot myself, met many interesting people and have become part of the local scene with requests to give talks and to advise people about getting into print.

Arthur L Clamp, 2001

Death of local historical author

'He was an incredible character who was just loved by everybody who knew him'

A WELL-loved Elburton author has died at the age of 68.

Arthur Clamp (pictured right), who was one of the West Country's most successful writers, died at St Luke's Hospice, Turnchapel, after losing his battle against cancer.

Tributes have been flooding in for a man who was known in the community as a prominent writer and outgoing person.

He produced more than 140 titles during his life, dealing with both fiction, fact and history, often discussing West Country topics that were close to his heart.

One of his most acclaimed books was *The Plymouth Blitz*, and he also won credit for *The Rise and Fall of the Bearings of Membland Hall*, set in Noss Mayo.

He achieved sales of between 7,000 and 9,000 books every year and it is estimated that he has sold over half a million books, covering the areas of Plymouth, Dartmoor, Exeter, Torbay and the South Hams.

Mr Clamp was born in Mitcham, Surrey, in 1932, and was the eldest of four children.

He moved to Devon in 1941 to avoid the London air-raids.

Mr Clamp trained as a printer in Exeter and also gained a teachers' certificate in 1959 from Garnet College in London.

Plymouth College of Art, however, was to prove to be Mr Clamp's working home for the following 32 years until 1991, when he retired as head of the printing department.

He had a great interest in travel and had visited the USA, Tanzania, China, Russia, Peru, as well as travelling across Europe, where he presented talks and slide shows on his experiences as a writer.

Mr Clamp was a member of Elburton Methodist Church for many years, superintendent of the Sunday school and editor of the church newsletter, as well as being involved in much charity work.

He was president of the Plymouth and District Field Club and an active member of the Elburton Residents' Association.

He enjoyed leading walks on Dartmoor and historical tours throughout the West Country.

Mr Clamp married his first wife, Rosemary, in 1956 and they had five children – Susan, Angela, Elizabeth, David and Steven – and she died in 1987. He also had 11 grandchildren.

He leaves a wife Christine, after remarrying in 1991, and her two children and three grandchildren.

'He was an incredible character who was just loved by everybody who knew him,' said his wife.

'He will be missed by his family, his friends, the people he worked with and just everybody who knew him through his books.'

More than 300 mourners attended his funeral at Elburton Methodist Church on Monday.

'The attendance was a celebration of his life – he would have found that really special. It shows his vibrancy and love of people,' said Mrs Clamp.

Steven Clamp added that his father was 'a well respected and loved man, missed by a great many people throughout the South West and far beyond'.

This newspaper article, published by the Evening Herald on 17th August 2001, forms a good record of his life. Just as he encourages us to learn more about local history, we encourage you to learn a little about him. For that reason, we have included these pages at the back of all the most recently republished books, in honour of his memory and recognition of his contribution to the community.

www.ingramcontent.com/pod-product-compliance
Lightning Source LLC
Chambersburg PA
CBHW061406070526
44584CB00031B/4174